LAR

Books should be returned or renewed by the last
date above. Renew by phone 03000 41 31 31 or
online www.kent.gov.uk/libs   SNF

CUSTOMER
SERVICE
EXCELLENCE

Kent
County
Council
kent.gov.uk

Libraries Registration & Archives

BRIGHT
IDEA
BOOKS

THE Universe
BEGAN WITH
A Bang:
COOL SPACE FACTS

by Kimberly M. Hutmacher

raintree
a Capstone company — publishers for children

Raintree is an imprint of Capstone Global Library Limited, a company incorporated in England and Wales having its registered office at 264 Banbury Road, Oxford, OX2 7DY – Registered company number: 6695582

www.raintree.co.uk
myorders@raintree.co.uk

Edited by Meg Gaertner
Designed by Becky Daum
Production by Colleen McLaren
Printed and bound in India

ISBN 978 1 4747 7459 8 (hardback)
ISBN 978 1 4747 8244 9 (paperback)

British Library Cataloguing in Publication Data
A full catalogue record for this book is available from the British Library.

Acknowledgements
We would like to thank the following for permission to reproduce photographs: iStockphoto: Magnilion, cover, Pobytov, cover; NASA: Goddard Space Flight Center, 5, 8–9, 16–17, 20–21, 23, Jet Propulsion Laboratory/California Institute of Technology, 7, 10–11, 13, Johns Hopkins University Applied Physics Laboratory/Southwest Research Institute/Jet Propulsion Laboratory/California Institute of Technology, 15, 28, Johnson Space Center, 17, Kim Shiflett/Kennedy Space Center, 27, Marshall Space Flight Center, 25, STScI/AURA/Jet Propulsion Laboratory/California Institute of Technology, 19, UCLA/MPS/DLR/IDA/Jet Propulsion Laboratory/California Institute of Technology, 14, USGS/Jet Propulsion Laboratory/California Institute of Technology, 12–13; Shutterstock Images: Allexxandar, 30–31, cover
Every effort has been made to contact copyright holders of material reproduced in this book. Any omissions will be rectified in subsequent printings if notice is given to the publisher.

We would like to thank Christine Gabrielse, PhD, Assistant Researcher in Earth, Space and Planetary Sciences, for her help with this book.

CONTENTS

WELCOME
to the
Universe

Space is filled with wonders. Stars explode. Some stars become **black holes**. There is a planet that smells like farts. The Moon has no wind. Welcome to the universe!

The Crab Nebula formed
after a star exploded.

CHAPTER 2

THE SOLAR System

The universe has more than 100 billion **galaxies**. One is the Milky Way. The **solar system** is in the Milky Way. At the solar system's centre is the Sun.

There are hundreds of billions of stars in the Milky Way galaxy.

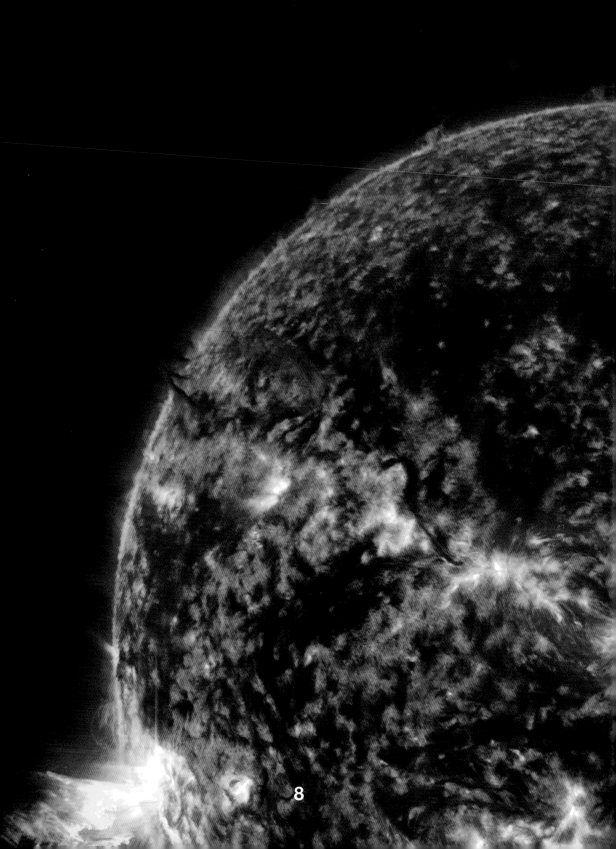

8

THE SUN

The Sun is a star. It is huge compared with Earth. Its **mass** makes up most of the solar system. But the Sun is small compared with other stars. The Sun has **solar storms**. A very strong wind blows out from the Sun. This can cause power cuts on Earth.

The Sun's core burns at about 15 million degrees Celsius (27 million degrees Fahrenheit).

EARTH

There are eight planets in the solar system. Earth is the third planet from the Sun. It has liquid water on its surface. None of the other planets do. Earth is the only planet known to support life.

Jupiter's Great Red Spot is a massive storm that has lasted for more than a century.

OTHER PLANETS

Jupiter is the largest planet. It is as big as 1,321 Earths put together! Venus is the hottest planet. It reaches 450 degrees Celsius (842 degrees Fahrenheit). Mercury is the smallest planet. Pluto is smaller. But Pluto is called a dwarf planet.

A GASSY PLANET

Uranus has clouds of hydrogen sulphide. This gas smells like farts.

Uranus was the first planet discovered by telescope.

DWARF PLANETS

Dwarf planets are similar to planets. They are round. They **orbit** the Sun. But they are smaller than Earth's Moon. There are five dwarf planets. Ceres orbits between Mars and Jupiter. Eris is very far from the Sun. It takes 557 Earth years to move around the Sun.

In 2015, Ceres became the first dwarf planet to be visited by spacecraft.

Pluto has red snow,
high mountains and
a blue sky.

OTHER OBJECTS IN THE SOLAR SYSTEM

Comets are made of ice and dust. Sometimes they get too close to the Sun. The Sun's heat turns the ice into gas. The comet disappears.

Moons orbit planets. People have landed on Earth's Moon. They have left footprints. Earth's Moon has no wind. The footprints will not be blown away. They will be there for millions of years.

This footprint was made during the Apollo 11 mission to the Moon in 1969.

CHAPTER 3

STARRY
Night

A star is a giant ball of gas. **Gravity** holds it together. No one knows how many stars there are. You might see 2,000 to 2,500 stars on a clear night. A star's light travels trillions of kilometres to reach Earth.

SEEING THE PAST

The North Star is 680 **light-years** away from Earth. Its light takes 680 years to reach Earth. Look at the star at night. You are seeing it as it looked 680 years ago!

Some stars explode and shoot out gas in all directions.

BLACK HOLES

A huge star explodes. Its centre collapses. A black hole forms. A huge amount of matter is in a very small space. Its gravity is strong. It pulls in nearby stars. Not even light can escape its pull. There are some massive black holes. They are billions of times bigger than the Sun.

There is a black hole at the centre of almost every galaxy.

NOT SO CLOSE

Black holes are not a danger for Earth. The nearest one is more than 20,000 light-years away.

CHAPTER 4

INTO THE
Dark

People can directly measure only 5 per cent of the universe. The other 95 per cent is a mystery. Scientists believe it is made up of two things. These are **dark matter** and **dark energy**. Scientists are not sure what these are. But they must exist for the universe to work.

The universe formed 13.8 billion years ago. It exploded into being. It has been expanding ever since. Dark energy acts against gravity. It has to exist for the universe to expand. Dark matter cannot be seen. But scientists can see its effects on gravity. It has to exist for galaxies to form.

Scientists think dark matter shapes how galaxies form and change over time.

CHAPTER 5

EXPLORING
Space

Astronauts visit space. Yuri Gagarin was the first person in space. He left Earth on 12 April 1961. Neil Armstrong was the first to walk on the Moon. He landed on 20 July 1969. Soon ordinary people may be able to visit and explore space.

Armstrong can be seen reflected in the helmet of his crewmate, Edwin Aldrin.

Companies are making tourist rockets. Blue Origin made a capsule. It can hold six people. A rocket will take it to space. It will go more than 100 kilometres (62 miles) above the Earth's surface. Riders will feel weightless. They will look out of windows and see space. The capsule will separate from the rocket. It has parachutes. It will slowly land on Earth. Someday you might visit space!

Riders will receive training before being cleared for lift-off in the Blue Origin crew capsule.

GLOSSARY

black hole
an area of space with such
a strong force of gravity that
nothing can escape

comet
an object made of gas, ice
and dust that orbits the Sun

dark energy
a force that must exist
to work against gravity
and explain the universe's
expansion

dark matter
a form of matter that takes up
space but cannot be seen

galaxy
a huge collection of stars and
other space objects that are
bound together by gravity

gravity
a force that pulls objects
with mass towards each other

light-year
the distance that light can
travel in one year, equal
to almost 9 trillion km (6
trillion miles)

mass
a measurement of how much
matter is in an object

orbit
to move in a set path around
another object

solar storm
strong solar winds released
by the Sun

solar system
the Sun and all of the space
objects bound to it by gravity,
including planets, asteroids
and comets

TRIVIA

1. There is a volcano on Mars. It is about three times larger than Earth's tallest mountain.

2. There is a planet called 55 Cancri e. Scientists think it is made of graphite and diamonds!

3. Scientists are looking for exoplanets. These are planets outside of the solar system. Scientists hope to find planets that could support life.

ACTIVITY

MARSHMALLOW CONSTELLATION

People look at the stars. They see shapes or patterns in the stars. These are called constellations. You can see some of the constellations here: https://stardate.org/nightsky/constellations.

You can make your own constellations. You will need a package of mini marshmallows and a box of toothpicks. The marshmallows will be the stars. The toothpicks will connect them. You can model your constellation after one you see on the website. Or you can make a new one!

FIND OUT MORE

Love learning facts about space? Find out more here.

Books

Do You Know About Space?, Sarah Cruddas (DK Children, 2017)

Space Discoveries (Marvellous Discoveries), Tamra Orr (Raintree 2019)

Totally Wacky Facts About Space (Mind Benders), Emma Carlson Berne (Raintree, 2015)

Websites

BBC Bitesize: The Solar System
www.bbc.com/bitesize/topics/zdrrd2p

DK Find Out!: Space
www.dkfindout.com/uk/space

National Geographic Kids: 10 Facts About Space!
www.natgeokids.com/uk/discover/science/space/ten-facts-about-space

INDEX